woodworking *with style*

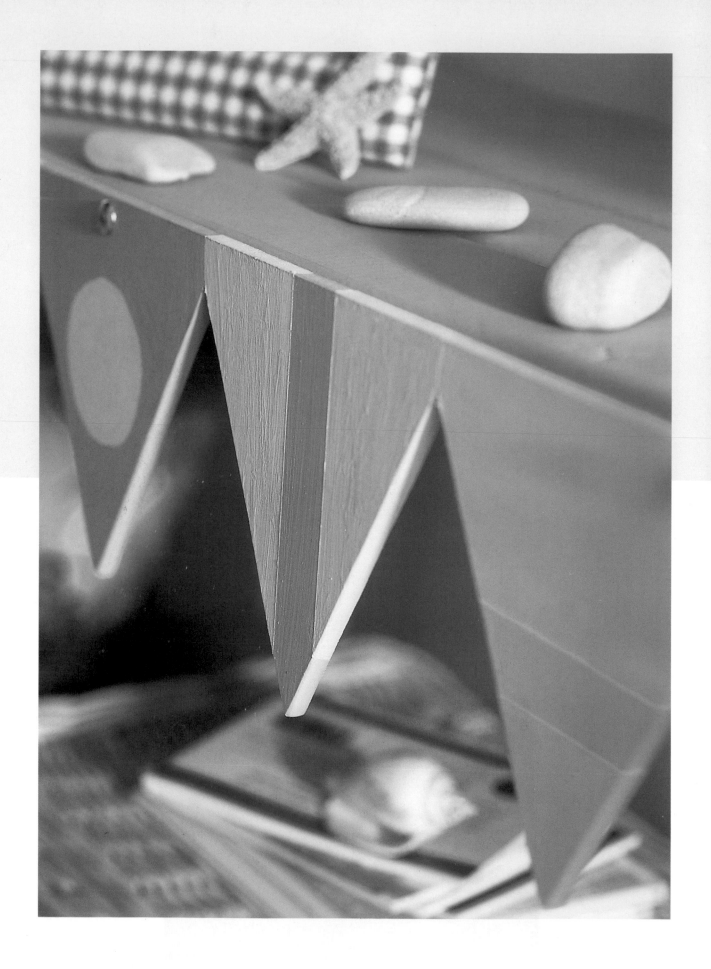

23
step-by-step
projects to
make over a
weekend

woodworking *with style*

Amanda Morrison
and
Cally Matthews

CICO BOOKS
London

c o n t

10 9 8 7 6 5 4 3 2 1
A CIP catalogue record for this book is available from the British Library
ISBN 1 903116 18 X

Photography by Lucinda Symons
Additional photography by Brian Hatton and Matthew Dickens
Styling by Denise Brock
Designed by Roger Daniels
Consultancy and editing by Ian Kearey
Photography managed by Kate Haxell

The authors wish to acknowledge Philip Haxell for his design contribution in the bathroom section.

Reproduction by Alliance Graphics, Singapore
Printed and bound in Italy by Editoriale Johnson

ents

Introduction

If, until now, your experience of wood-working books has been technical manuals with frightening diagrams and lists of specialist equipment, then think again. Wood-working with Style throws away all those pre-conceptions, and instead is a celebration of the versatility of wood and MDF.

It doesn't matter if you don't know one end of a jigsaw from the other. This book includes some very simple ideas that are ideal for beginners. These are the perfect way to build confidence so that, after a time, you will feel ready to progress onto more involved pieces.

Like most creative pursuits, once you get the hang of it, woodworking is great fun. It's also very rewarding to be able to stand back from a completed project and say 'all my own work'.

What about the cost? If you decide to rush off to your local DIY store and invest in all the latest equipment, woodworking can certainly become quite expensive. But the good news is that you don't need all the latest gizmos and gadgets: a few key tools are enough to get you started (see 'Toolbox' on page 8). And when it comes to pricier items like power drills or jigsaws, try borrowing or hiring them before you buy. Alternatively, split the cost with a friend who shares your interest. That way you can get a feel for using equipment without incurring a lot of expense.

In the past, woodworking was seen as a specifically male interest, but that is no longer true. The equipment available today is much lighter and easier to manage than before. As project designs are becoming more creative, and the popularity of home improvement continues to grow, woodworking now appeals to everyone as never before. And if you take a look down the power tool aisle of your local DIY store, you'll notice that manufacturers are in on the act too, developing compact designs with just as much punch as their weightier predecessors. What are you waiting for?

A few inspiring ideas, of course – and that's what you will find here. The projects in this book are not only simple to make but look really smart too. They are divided into chapters, each one featuring a different room. The designs vary in scale but are all quite straightforward. Of course, once you become more confident, you can adapt or modify them to suit your own style and needs.

Whatever you do, remember to enjoy the challenge – and make safety a priority.

Safety

It goes without saying that safety is a key issue. Always follow these basic rules and use your common sense. It is never worth the risk of taking short cuts where safety is concerned.

● Always wear a mask and goggles when cutting wood or MDF, and work in a well-ventilated room if possible.

● When using power tools, follow the manufacturer's instructions carefully. Read them through once or twice before you begin, and if you feel that you are making a mistake or going off course, simply stop, sort yourself out and start again.

● Keep tools clean, and make sure that you use sharp blades and drill bits.

● Never leave a power tool running while you do something else, even if it's only going to take a second. Always turn it off.

● Electrical cables can be dangerous, so keep an eye open and be careful not to trip over them. This is especially true where extension leads are concerned.

● Wear gloves when dealing with wire or other sharp edges.

● Use adhesives carefully. Follow the instructions on the packet and make sure that you select the correct glue for the materials with which you are working. If in doubt, ask at your local DIY store.

● Secure items firmly when cutting or drilling.

● Tie long hair back and remove all loose jewellery. Make sure that your clothes don't hang loosely – roll up your sleeves to work!

● Don't be put off by these safety pointers. They are there to help you, not to alarm, but the accidents that do happen are preventable nine times out of ten, so they are worth bearing in mind and following.

MDF

MDF (medium-density fibreboard) is easy to work with and relatively inexpensive, and its smooth surface is a dream for paint finishes – no wonder it's so popular. It pays to respect your materials, however, and caution should be used when working with MDF. Dust caused by cutting MDF can irritate, so always wear a mask and work in a well-ventilated area. The average home woodworker is unlikely to be affected, because contact with the dust is likely to be relatively minor – but take care anyway.

Measurements

When embarking on a project, decide on either metric or imperial measurements and stick to them. Do not switch between measurement systems as, although every effort has been made to ensure consistency, the finished project may be affected.

Toolbox

This set of tools and equipment will get you started. Before you begin a new project, check the tools required so that you have everything to hand – there's nothing more frustrating than having to stop halfway through a step because you don't have the necessary equipment.

Invest in a decent-sized toolbox to store all your gear. These boxes are very inexpensive and can be found in a variety of sizes.

Finally, take care of your tools. If you keep them clean and free from dust, they will last longer and continue to perform well.

Pencil

Safety ruler

Compasses

Try square

Scissors

Craft knife

Retractable tape measure

Mitre block

Spirit level

Jigsaw

Staple gun

Tenon saw

Crosscut saw

Hand drill

Flat bit

Straight bit

Countersink bit

Hole saw

Power drill

Pliers

Selection
of nails
and screws

Corner plates

Flat plate

Nail (centre) punch

Bradawl

Wood adhesive

Epoxy resin
adhesive

Filler knife

Cross-head screwdriver

Flat-head screwdriver

Claw hammer   Pin hammer

Adhesive gun and
gap-filling adhesive

Mitre clamp

Flat paintbrush

Stippling brush

Artist's brush

Sanding
paper in
several grades,
including wet and
dry, with sanding block

G-clamp

Techniques

1 Measuring
To measure from an edge with a tape, hook the end of the tape over the edge to hold it in place and mark the required measurement with a pencil. For a line parallel to the edge, continue this process by sliding the tape down along the edge and marking again. Always get someone to help when measuring long distances.

For joining measured points, use a steel safety ruler to join rows of pencil marks. Safety rulers enable you to get a good grip and are usually marked in metric and imperial measurements. Use a soft pencil for drawing lines so the marks can be erased quite easily.

2 Using a try square to mark parallel lines
This device makes marking parallel lines a straightforward job. Simply rest the top of the try on the top edge of the piece on which you are working, and draw a pencil line along the metal edge.

3 Marking diagonals to find the centre of a rectangle
To find the true centre of a rectangular or square piece of wood, draw two diagonal pencil lines from corner to corner. The point where the lines bisect is the centre of the piece of wood.

4 Waxing saw teeth
This helps to lubricate the saw and thus make the cutting action smoother. Soap is an alternative that works just as well, but be warned – lubricating will only help sharp blades and is not a magical technique for making blunt blades good.

5 Cutting with a tenon saw

Make one or two cuts to create a small notch before you start in earnest. That way, the blade will be more stable and you will therefore make a better job.

6 Cutting with a crosscut saw

Because a crosscut saw is longer and does not have strengthening along the top, you have to take care that the blade does not flex while you are sawing – practice will pay dividends here.

7 Cutting a straight line in a mitre block

Mitre blocks are an invaluable means of ensuring that a straight line is really straight. Simply slot the saw through the parallel notches on either side and saw down through your length of wood. Clamping a mitre block in a workbench gives it extra stability and makes the work easier.

8 Cutting a mitre in a mitre block

Mitred edges are cut at 45 degrees so they form neat corners when joined together. Use the same principle as you do for cutting straight lines, but this time slot the blade of the saw through one of the two notches that are diagonally opposite one another.

9 Cutting a wavy line with a jigsaw

If you haven't used a jigsaw before, they behave in much the same way as a sewing machine, but with a blade instead of a needle. The key to accurate cutting is to make sure that the surface is firmly secured (in a workbench, for example) – and to take your time. Simply guide the blade along the line that you have drawn, and if you go off course for any reason, don't panic, but stop before restarting in the right direction. Minor mistakes can be smoothed away with sandpaper. For the best results, the blade should always be sharp.

10 Cutting out an internal circle

After drawing the circle, drill a hole a few centimetres away from its edge at the top right if you are right-handed. You will be cutting from right to left in an anticlockwise direction. If you are left-handed, drill the hole top left and cut clockwise.

11 Cutting out an internal square

This technique is very simple once you know how. Before you start cutting, drill four holes, one at each corner of the square – the holes should sit inside the pencil marks and be wide enough to accommodate the jigsaw's blade. Start at one corner and work along one side until you reach the next corner. You may have to unclamp the wood and move it around after cutting each side to make it easier to work. Always cut in the same direction.

12 Cutting thin dowelling

With very thin dowelling, mark where you want to cut and hold a sharp craft-knife blade over the mark. Roll the dowel until it cuts in two. With slightly wider dowelling, use the same method to score the wood, but snap it in two and sand to finish.

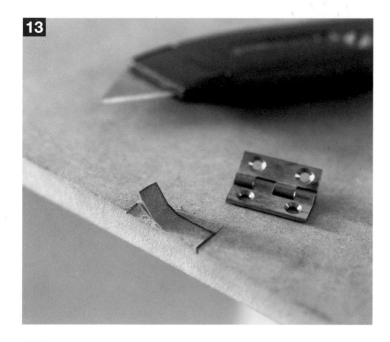

13 Cutting rebated hinges

The surface of rebated hinges should sit flush with the surrounding wood or MDF. Use the hinges themselves as a template and draw around their outline in pencil. With a sharp craft knife, carefully score along these lines, then, working the blade horizontally, remove a fine layer at a time until you have reached the correct depth. If you remove too much, you can rectify the mistake by applying a fine layer of filler.

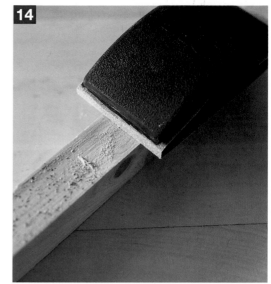

14 Sanding a flat surface

A sanding block makes it easier to cover a large area and prevents the danger of friction burns. There are several types of block, although they all do basically the same job. Sandpaper comes in different grades. In general, rough grades are used first and followed by finer ones to give a completely smooth. Wet and dry paper is made for use between coats of paint or varnish and almost polishes the surface, making it completely smooth. Always finish with a coat of paint or varnish, however (unless you are distressing a surface) as the action of sanding will affect the finished colour. For the best results, apply paint in the same direction as you sanded.

15 Sanding a rounded edge

Use the same priciple as before, but this time angle the sanding block so that it removes the hard edge of the wood. This is easier if the wood is properly secured.

16 Sanding a corner

Again, this technique removes the hard edges, this time at the corner points. This takes little time and is a wise safety precaution, particularly on lower-level items such as benches or tables.

17 Sanding the inside of a circle

Customize a length of dowelling or a pencil by wrapping it in sandpaper so that you can work it around the diameter of the cut circle quite easily.

18 Using a bradawl

This tool ensures accuracy whether you are fixing screws or nails, or making a pilot hole for a fine drill bit. Mark the exact centre of the hole that you want to make with a pencil cross, and dig the pointed end of the bradawl in firmly where the lines bisect. This will give you a good starting point.

19 Drilling a hole

Again, mark the exact centre of the hole that you want to drill with a pencil cross. Hold the drill perpendicular to the surface so that you are not drilling at an angle. If the bit has a point, ensure that this sits on the centre of the cross before you start to drill. Start with a fine drill bit and work your way up if necessary. For the best results, make sure that you get your full weight behind the drill.

20 Putting tape on a drill bit

If you wish to drill through wood to a specified depth, rather than all the way through, simply measure from the point of the bit to your required point, and bind the area beyond with masking tape. Drill slowly, and stop when the tape is flush with the surface of the wood, as you will have reached the correct level.

21 Countersinking a screw

a) Do this on surfaces where it is important that screw holes are not visible. A countersink bit creates a hole with sloped sides into which the countersink screw fits, with its head below the surface of the wood.

b) Check that you have the correct size of screw for the job before you start. It should be long enough to comfortably fit through all of the top layer and at least half of the bottom layer of wood.

22 Filling a countersunk screw head

a) The sunken screw head sits with its head a little way below the surface of the wood.

b) The small gap can be filled with wood filler, smoothed over to the level of the wood. If you are using screws that are not galvanized, dab a touch of PVA or oil-based paint on the head before applying filler, to prevent rusting.

c) When dry, simply sand the filler with very fine paper so that the original hole is virtually undetectable.

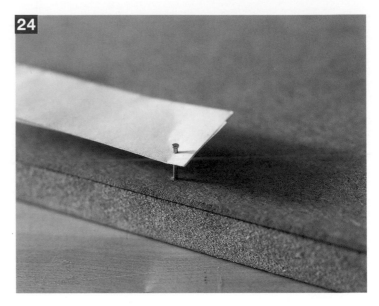

23 Nailing two pieces of wood together

Check that you have the right nails for the job before you start. Too short and they will not be secure: too long and they will come through the other side of the wood. If in doubt, check at your local DIY store or timber merchant.

The nail should be hammered in straight. Use a hammer that is a comfortable weight and not too heavy for the size of the nails that you are using.

24 Holding a nail with paper

With smaller nails in particular, it can be tricky getting started without hammering your fingers! If you push the nail through a length of paper or fine card, you can hold it steady from a few centimetres away and get on with the job safely.

25 Punching a nail

For a neat finish, use a nail (centre) punch to drive the head of the nail down below the surface of the wood. Hold the punch perpendicular to the nail and drive it in using a hammer. You can fill the hole as for a countersunk screw head.

26 Covering a hammer

When hammering in upholstery tacks or anything with a decorative head that might get damaged, it is wise to bandage your hammer with a scrap of soft fabric. Secure it with a length of cord or an elastic band.

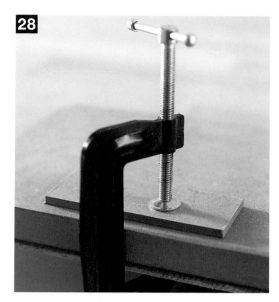

27 Glueing and clamping

Always follow the instructions on the adhesive that you buy, as some will vary.

a) Apply glue to one or both of the sides to be joined (this may depend on the type of glue you use).

28 Clamping and protecting surfaces

Clamping is a very effective method of holding joints firmly whilst glue dries, but clamps' hard metal surfaces can sometimes damage the wood when applied at pressure. To prevent this from happening, particularly on soft wood like pine, simply slot in a thin offcut of wood or MDF for protection.

b) Use clamps to firmly secure the two pieces that are being joined. Remove any glue that has squeezed up from the joint with a cloth straight away, before it has a chance to harden.

29 Masking for stripes

Masking tape guarantees a neat, professional edge to any paint finish and is the ideal way of creating perfect stripes. Mark out in pencil where you want the stripes to go. Then run masking tape along the marks' length, checking that the tape edge aligns exactly with the pencil line. Press down firmly all the way along to remove any tiny air bubbles before starting to paint. It is easiest to work one colour at a time, so make sure that you have masked off the correct stripes. Masking tape is available in several thicknesses, so choose one that's right for the scale of the project and the size of your brush.

The Hall

Hallways give the first impression of your home, yet the lack of space can make them a problem to furnish and decorate. A few essential items of furniture combined with a clever colour scheme, however, will ensure that your hall gives a warm welcome, whatever its size.

Console table

Few people have the luxury of a spacious hallway, so any hall furniture has to work hard to earn its place. This compact console is no exception. Customized from a set of wooden drawers available from high street stores, the finished table takes up little space yet is just the right size for a few essential items. If space is limited elsewhere, you can also adapt the design to make consoles in bedrooms or bathrooms.

you will need

- 1 Standard two-drawer box
- 1 piece softwood 680 x 22 x 15 mm (26¾ x ⅞ x ⅝ in)
- 2 metal legs with circular brackets and screws
- Mitre block
- Handsaw
- Wood glue
- G-clamps
- Power drill and flat bit
- Screws
- Screwdriver
- Jigsaw
- 2 pieces 15mm (⅝ in) MDF the same diameter as leg brackets
- Bradawl
- 2 handles
- Pearl-finish paint or emulsion paint plus pearl-effect top coat
- Masking tape
- Wall plugs and screws

1 Use the mitre block and handsaw to mitre the ends of the softwood so that it measures 680mm (26¾ in) at its longest point. This forms the batten that is fitted to the base of the console table and attaches it to the wall.

3 Use the metal bracket that attaches the leg to the table as a template to cut out two MDF circles. It is necessary to build up a little extra depth like this, otherwise the screws would drive through the wood into the box, making it impossible to open the drawers. Sand the circle edges smooth.

2 Turn the drawer box upside down, place the batten against the back edge of the base and mark the ends so that it sits exactly in the middle. Drill three equally spaced pilot holes through the batten, then turn it onto the next face and drill three more equally spaced holes for the wall screws – make sure that the two sets of holes are not too near each other. Apply glue to the batten and clamp it into place. Drive screws into the base. When the glue is dry, remove the clamps.

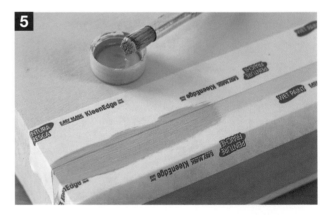

4 Apply strong wood adhesive to the MDF circles and position them on the base of the table, one at each corner – the edge of the circles should be around 10–18mm (⅜–¾in) from the edges of the base. Secure with clamps and allow to dry.

5 Paint the box with two coats of emulsion, making sure that the first coat is completely dry before starting the second. Turn the drawers around so that they have a complete front – to prevent them from sticking, it is best to paint only the front part of the drawers and leave the sides unfinished. To give guide lines for painting a decorative striped border around the edge, apply masking tape to give a 12mm (½in) wide line around 18mm (¾in) in from the front and back edges. Paint and leave to dry before repeating the process on the two shorter edges. Repeat, this time with a narrower line in a contrasting colour.

6 Position the leg brackets on the MDF circles on the base, and use a bradawl to mark the screw holes. Drill out the holes and use the screws provided in the kit to screw the circular metal leg bracket onto the MDF.

design tip

● You might like to adapt this basic idea to create a small-scale dressing table. Simply hang a mirror on the wall behind and you've got it. Don't be tempted to amass a lot of clutter, however, as the table isn't strong enough to bear much weight.

7 Attach the legs, following the instructions with the kit. With an assistant, carefully position the finished table against the wall so that the legs are square on the ground. Mark a horizontal line on the wall, using the underside of the batten as a guide and checking it with a spirit level. Use the pilot holes in the batten to mark for wall plugs, then remove the table. Drill and insert the wall plugs, then reposition the table and drive in the wall screws through the batten.

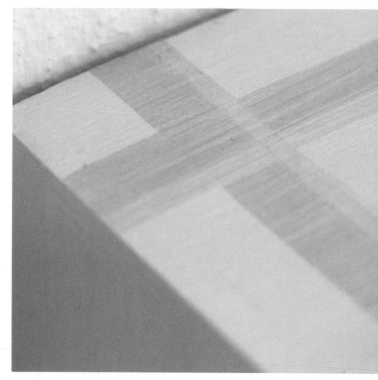

8 Drill any necessary holes, then screw a handle into the painted front of each drawer to complete your console table.

For a glamorous finish, use a specialist paint that gives a pearly lustre. You could even experiment with using both plain and pearly finishes.

Radiator cover

A lot more fun – both to look at and make – than the average radiator cover, this version knocks spots off traditional styles. The basic construction is straightforward but if you are new to working with wood, it is best to start on a relatively small size. And once you feel confident, why not experiment with different finishing touches on the front panel to give your radiator cover a really individual look?

dimensions

No dimensions have been given for the pieces here, as they will obviously be taken from the size of the radiator that you wish to cover. Measure it carefully, taking note of any valves and pipes, and remember to include the depth – how far out from the wall it stands. When you have completed your measurements, add 10–19 mm (⅜–¾ in) all around so that the cover stands a little way from the surface of the radiator. Pipework usually runs close to the wall and doesn't present much of a problem. You will need easy access to valves, however – cutting a small section out of the side is usually the simplest way to reach the valve.

you will need

Front
- 1 piece MDF

Sides
- 2 pieces MDF

Top
- 1 piece MDF
- 2 softwood battens
- Jigsaw
- Power drill with hole saw and flat bits
- Sandpaper
- Steel rule

- Pencil
- Compasses
- Bradawl
- Metal studs
- Hammer with fabric to cover head
- Screws for battens
- Corner braces with short screws
- Screwdriver
- Gloss paint and primer (optional)
- Emulsion paint and water-based varnish (optional) and paintbrush

1 Mark two sections along the base edge of the front piece to form legs, using a pair of compasses to create curves. The measurements and the number of legs will depend on the size of your radiator. If you aren't sure what will look best, experiment on a cardboard template. For a long radiator like the one shown here, a central leg is a good idea; on smaller radiators, side legs alone are fine. The height of the legs should be roughly one-fifth to one-sixth the overall height of the radiator. Draw a pencil line on the front piece of MDF, parallel to the base, making sure that the base of the radiator will not show. Use a jigsaw to cut out the section or sections, and sand the cut edge until it is smooth.

2 Use different sizes of hole saw attachment on a power drill to cut random holes in the front piece, working from the outer face inwards. If you aren't sure about how the pattern will look, plot it out on graph paper before you start. Alternatively, stick round pieces of paper of various sizes on the MDF and move them around to give you an idea. Sand the edges of the holes.

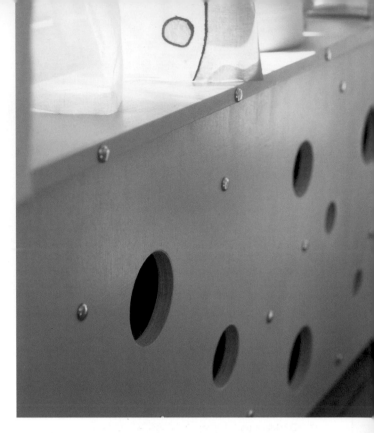

3 Gently sand, dust and paint the front, side and top pieces. You can either use primer and an oil-based paint such as eggshell or gloss, or emulsion paint with an oil-based varnish on top. Allow to dry completely.

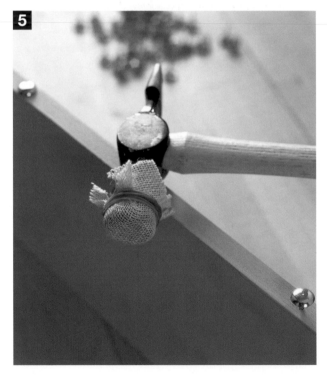

4 To further decorate the front piece, use a bradawl to make small random pilot holes for metal studs. Before driving in the studs, cover the hammer head with a piece of fabric as shown, to avoid damaging the stud heads.

design tips

● Decorative, yet practical too, wire meshes and grilles are perfect for radiator covers.
● Alternatively, for a more rustic look, you could try gardeners' chicken wire which comes in a variety of gauges and is very inexpensive.

5 Repeat step 4 for the front edge of the top piece, this time making the pilot holes at regular intervals. To prevent the wood from splitting, you can enlarge the bradawl holes with a small drill bit before hammering in the studs.

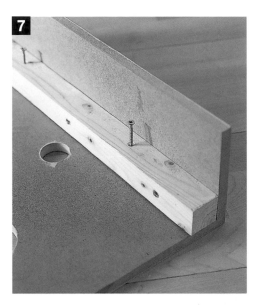

7 Position the sides and battens against the front piece as shown, and repeat step 6 to attach the sides to the front. Again, make sure that the screws you use are long enough to go through the batten and into the front, but not so long that they break out on the other side.

6 The softwood battens that attach the sides to the front are the same length as the side pieces of MDF. Mark and drill regularly spaced guide holes through the battens; the screws used must be long enough to bite into the sides without breaking out through the outer face. Lay one side down onto its painted face, position a batten so its edge is exactly along the side edge, and drive in the screws through the guide holes. Repeat for the other batten and side piece.

8 Lay the top piece on its painted side. Position the assembled sides and front in place, then position corner braces, to hold the front and top together, at regular intervals along the meeting edges – again, the number of plates depends on the size of the cover. Mark and bradawl the screw holes through the plates, then drive in very short, stubby screws that do not protrude through the MDF.

Once you have got the hang of the basic construction of the radiator cover, there is no end to the effects you can create on the front panel. A simple grid of rectangular shapes in varying widths, backed with muslin, can look extremely effective.

Letter rack

Every hall should have a handy letter rack like this to help prevent papers and keys from getting lost. Don't be put off by the number of steps – it is quite simple to make, although you will need to work methodically as some of the techniques are a bit fiddly. If you prefer to change the shape of the rack ends, all you need do is draw your own template. When your rack is complete and in place, you'll wonder how you ever managed without it.

you will need

- 1 piece 2mm MDF 990 x 340 mm (39 x 13⅜in)
- Steel ruler
- 1 piece paper 340 x 150 mm (13⅜ x 6 in)
- Craft knife
- Small tenon saw
- Pencil
- Dressmaker's pins
- Set square
- Try square
- 2 pieces softwood 690 x 33 x 22 mm (27¼ x 1¼ x ⅞in)
- Wood glue
- G-clamps
- Panel pins
- 3 lengths 10mm (⅜in) diameter dowelling 440mm (17⅜in) long
- Power drill and 10 mm (⅜in) flat bit
- Emulsion paint
- Sandpaper
- Fine beading

1 Draw a line 150 mm (6 in) down from – and parallel to – the top of the hardboard. Repeat at the base. To make a template, fold the piece of paper in half lengthways and trace half of the curved design from the diagram onto it (see Templates). Cut along the line that you have drawn, open the paper out and place it in position on the hardboard, with the steel rule on the pencil line. Draw around the paper shape at the top and base, and use a sharp craft knife to cut out the design.

2 Next, you need to measure the hardboard and create a grid of pencil lines to act as a guide for the three flaps. This isn't difficult, just a little time-consuming – use a try square to ensure that the lines are parallel. Don't be tempted to rush the job: the old adage 'Measure twice and cut once' is the best guide.

3 The three inner rectangles that you have drawn will form the flaps in which you can store letters and papers. With a craft knife, cut along the top edge and two sides of each of the three flaps. Leave the base lines intact.

4 Stick a dressmaker's pin through each of the corners where the cut side lines join the base of the flaps, making sure that the points emerge on the other side. The pins will provide you with an accurate guide for the next step.

design tip

● To disguise the cracked hardboard at the base of each flap, cut a very fine length of beading to the width of the rack and glue it in place.

5 Turn the hardboard over so that the back of the rack is facing upwards. You should be able to see the sharp ends of two pins sticking through at the base of each flap. Score lightly with a craft knife between these two points to break the outer layer of board to enable the flap to pull forward slightly. Repeat for each flap and then remove the pins.

6 Cut to length two battens to run down either side of the rack and hold the lengths of dowelling. Set a set square to an angle over 45 degrees and draw this angle on each end of both battens, ensuring that all the angles are the same. Use the tenon saw to cut the ends, and smooth with sandpaper.

8 Clean up the holes with sandpaper. Glue and clamp the battens in place and, from the back of the hardboard, hammer panel pins in to secure the joins. Allow to dry.

7 Place one of the battens flat in position on the MDF rack. Measure 50 mm (2 in) up from the base of each flap and mark this accurately on the batten in pencil. These marks form the centre points of the holes for the dowelling. Sandwich the battens together to ensure that the holes line up, then drill through each of the pencil marks using a flat bit.

9 Lightly sand and dust the whole rack and then paint it, including the edges of the hardboard, with emulsion. Remember to paint the inside of the flaps for a smart finish. Allow to dry.

10 Make a pencil mark for the notches around 10 mm (⅜ in) in from either end of each length of dowelling. Carefully score a fine line along the mark with a craft knife, then cut out a V-shaped notch with the knife until you have an indentation all round. Smooth the whole length of dowelling lightly with fine sandpaper. Slide the lengths of dowelling through the holes.

The Living Room

One of the most public rooms in the house – and the one that has to be the most versatile – the living room may be used for entertaining friends, relaxing with a good book or simply unwinding in front of the television. All this can make choosing furniture a tall order. Comfort and function are equally important – not forgetting style. The simple pieces on the following pages not only look good, but will prove extremely useful too. And like all classic designs, they will never date: simply repaint them for a fresh, new look when you want to ring the changes.

Fireplace

Traditionally, the hearth has always been the heart of the home. In many older homes, however, fireplaces have either been boarded over or removed altogether, and many modern homes were built without fireplaces. This elegant surround will help reinstate a focal point in your living room – even if you don't have a real fire, you can create a stunning display with candles or flowers – and although it is on a large scale, it is remarkably easy to make. Take it a step at a time, and enlist the help of a friend as an extra pair of hands.

you will need

Inner section
- Two pieces wood or MDF 700 x 200 x 19mm (27½ x 8 x ¾ in)
- One piece wood or MDF 900 x 300 x 18mm (35½ x 11¾ x ¾ in)

Outer section
- Two pieces wood or MDF 1200 x 200 x 18mm (47¼ x 8 x ¾ in)
- One piece wood or MDF 800 x 300 x 18mm (31½ x 11¾ x ¾ in)

Sides
- Two pieces wood or MDF 1200 x 100 x 18mm (47¼ x 4 x ¾ in)

Mantel shelf
- (Top) One piece wood or MDF 1275 x 190 x 18mm (50¼ x 7½ x ¾ in)
- (Front) One piece wood or MDF 1300 x 50 x 18mm (51¼ x 2 x ¾ in)
- (Sides) Two pieces wood or MDF 190 x 50 x 18mm (7½ x 2 x ¾ in)
- Bradawl
- Screwdriver
- Countersunk wood screws 13 x 4 mm (½ x ⅛ in)
- Eight 125mm (5 in) mending plates
- Wood glue
- Emulsion paint
- Oil-based paint and flat paintbrush
- Mitre clamps
- Fine nails
- Hammer
- Centre punch
- Wood filler and filler knife
- Sandpaper and sanding block

1 The fireplace is formed from two inverted U shapes with a mantel shelf along the top. To make the inner U section, lay the two short pieces (the legs) against the long one, setting the long one across the top of the shorter pair. Make sure the side edges meet exactly, then place two flat plates across each joint, angled for strength. Use a bradawl to mark the screw holes. Apply glue to the joining edges, position them accurately and screw the meeting plates in place. Leave to dry.

2 Now make the outer section – this time, however, the middle piece slots in between the two legs instead of lying along the top of them. Lay out the pieces as before, this time making sure that there is at least a 125mm (5in) gap between the bottom of the middle section and the flat plates, to allow for the inner section when the two frames are joined together. Apply glue, drive in the screws and leave to dry.

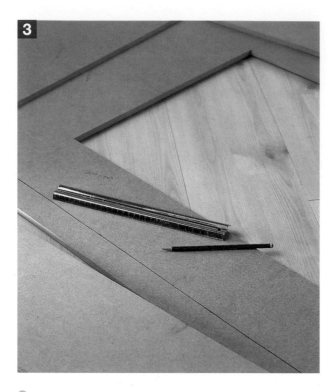

3 Before you join the outer and inner sections together to create the front of the fireplace, you need to make sure that the sections fit squarely onto one another. Lay the inner section on its back, then measure 50mm (2in) in from the outer edges and mark this along each leg. Join the marks to make a line along each leg.

4 Now line up the inner edges of the outside section with the marks that you have just drawn on the inner frame. Check carefully that both sections are square, then apply glue all around the three edges where the inner and outer sections overlap. Fit the sections together and allow to dry. **Inset:** When the glue has dried, countersink fine nails at 100mm (4in) intervals along the inner edge of the outer section. Use a centre punch to push the nail heads below the surface of the wood, then fill the holes with a little wood filler. Allow to dry, then sand the filler smooth with the wood surface.

design tips

● To avoid confusion when assembling the sections, mark on each piece of wood the section for which it is intended.

● Unless you are very adept, ask your local timber merchant to cut the wood for you. The cuts should avoid as much wastage as possible.

● If you are making the surround to fit a specific opening, you will have to modify the dimensions. If in doubt, trace the pieces onto large sheets of brown paper before you start ordering or cutting wood.

● Wooden battens or metal braces are the most common methods of securing fireplaces to a wall, but the best method will depend on the material from which your wall is built. Check with your local hardware store for advice on specific materials and fixing methods.

● You can create a hearth from wood, slate or marble. Look out for offcuts at your local stonemason.

5 Select the two narrow side pieces and check that they are an exact fit along the edges of the outer sections. Glue them into position as shown, and secure with mitre clamps. When dry, secure the join with nails from the front, then punch the nails down, fill and sand as before.

6 The shelf section is made from four pieces of wood – a top, front and two sides. Check that the sides fit on the outside edges of the shelf, then apply glue, position the sides and clamp them in place. Nail, punch down, fill and sand as before.

7 When the top and sides are dry, position them on their back edges and check the front for fit. Attach it in the same way as before. This time you will not be able to use mitre clamps, but you should be able to manage without as long as you work carefully at each stage of the process.

8 Place the mantel shelf in position on the main frame, making sure that there is a 50mm (2in) overhang at either end. Centre the shelf, apply glue and clamp it in place. Drive three nails on either side through the shelf top into the frame side pieces. Punch the nails down to countersink them, then fill and sand as before. Fill and sand any gaps in the finished fireplace, then prime with emulsion paint and paint with oil-based paint.

Display boxes

Once you get the hang of making these handy little display boxes, you won't want to stop – and it is easy to see why. Each box does not take long to make and can be painted and re-painted to go with any colour scheme. The boxes look great mounted on the wall, either individually or in groups or rows, showing off your favourite possessions. They also make great gifts for family and friends.

you will need

Sides
- 2 pieces MDF
  200 x 150 x 15 mm
  (8 x 6 x ⅝ in)

Top and base
- 2 pieces MDF
  170 x 150 x 15 mm
  (6¾ x 6 x ⅝ in)
- Wood glue
- Mitre clamps
- Sandpaper and
  sanding block

- Steel rule
- Pencil
- Hammer
- Fine nails
- Centre punch
- Wood filler and
  filler knife
- Emulsion paint
- Water-based
  varnish
- Flat paintbrush

1 Dry assemble the box on its back with the top and base held inside its sides. Mark the meeting edges and outer faces of all four of the pieces. Before putting the pieces together, chamfer the outer edges of the top and bottom sections along the depth of the box. This helps to mask any slight inaccuracy in the finished, shaped pieces.

2 Apply glue along the top inside end of one side piece, then position it and the meeting edge of the top piece together in a L shape, holding them in place with mitre clamps until completely dry. Repeat with the other side piece, this time with the glue along the bottom meeting edge, and the base.

design tips

- As these boxes are quite small, they are an excellent way of using up left-over paint or tester pots.
- When you get the hang of making the boxes, you can experiment with different dimensions. Don't be tempted to make them too big, however – they work best on a small scale.

3 Use a ruler and pencil to mark a line across the sides, 8mm (5⁄16in) from each end. Mark for three equally spaced nails along each of these lines. Hammer in fine nails to strengthen the glued joints, then glue, assemble and clamp the two L-shaped pieces together to create a square box. Allow to dry, then hammer in nails to strengthen the 'new' joints.

4 Use a centre punch and hammer to push down the heads of the nails so that they lie below the surface of the MDF. Fill the holes with wood filler, allow to dry and sand smooth. Paint the boxes with emulsion, allow to dry and finish with a couple of coats of water-based varnish.

Coffee table

Whether you want to make this table from scratch or prefer to customize an existing one, by incorporating test tubes into the design, you will never have to look for a vase again!

The simplest ideas really are the best. A plain table has been given a contemporary twist with the addition of nine drilled holes and a set of glass test tubes (available from good chemists and pharmaceutical suppliers). Hey presto! An instant new look – and one that can be changed as often as you change the floral arrangement (you can also use dried flowers). Take time in deciding how many holes you want – and where you want to position them. You might prefer a more random effect or perhaps a wavy line, bisecting the table diagonally from corner to corner. Once you have plotted exactly where you want to drill, mark each spot carefully. Err on the side of caution: it is easy to enlarge a hole that's too small, but virtually impossible to tighten a hole that has been drilled too big.

you will need

Top
- 1 piece MDF 675 x 675 x 19mm
  (26⅝ x 26⅝ x ¾in)

Rails
- 4 pieces softwood 535 x 45 x 19mm
  (21 x 1¾ x ¾in)
- 8 corner braces 38 x 30 x 25mm
  (1½ x 1⅛ x 1in)
- 32 woodscrews 13mm (½in) long

Legs
- 4 pieces softwood 430 x 45 x 45mm
  (17 x 1¾ x 1¾in)
- 8 corner braces 38 x 30 x 10mm
  (1½ x 1⅛ x ⅜in)
- 32 woodscrews 16mm (⅝in) long
- 9 glass 19mm (¾in) diameter test tubes
- Straightedge
- Pencil
- Hand saw or jigsaw
- Power drill and 19mm (¾in) flat bit
- Bradawl
- Screwdriver
- Try square
- Wood glue
- Mitre clamps
- Abrasive paper and sanding block
- Primer and emulsion or gloss paint

1 Cut the table top to size with a crosscut saw or jigsaw, making sure that the corners are true right angles. Find the centre of of the top by drawing corner-to-corner diagonals, then measure and draw edge-to-edge lines through the centre in both directions. Draw two more lines, 70mm (2¾in) on either side of one horizontal line. Where these lines meet the diagonals, join them to make a square.

2 Where the lines intersect, use a 19mm (¾in) flat bit to drill a hole at each meeting point. Sand the insides of the nine holes, check that a 19mm (¾in) diameter test tube will fit, and adjust the holes as required.

3 Cut the four rails to length, ensuring that the ends are cut square. Measure and mark 85mm (3⅜in) from each end. Hold a rail brace with its outer edge against each mark in turn, with the 30mm (1⅛in) edge against the wood, and use a bradawl to make pilot screw holes – it is vital that the 'L' is flush with the bottom edge of the rail. Screw the brace in place, using the 13mm (½in) long woodscrews.

4 On the bottom face of the table top, use a try square to mark 70mm (2¾in) from each end at the corners, and a straightedge to mark a line 40mm (1⅝in) in from, and parallel to, each edge. Position each rail in turn with the outside edges on the lines, bradawl pilot holes and screw into place – use a try square to check that the rails meet the top at right angles.

5 Cut the legs to length, and make sure that both ends are cut square. Apply wood glue to one end of a leg and each end of two rails at a corner. Push the leg to meet the rails, and use mitre clamps to hold it in place, checking the right angle between leg and top with a try square. Repeat for the other legs and leave to dry.

design tips

● You can use gloss or emulsion paints for a solid colour finish to match your room.
● Use your imagination to create other finishes – combining colours, painting stripes or patterns, using spray paints, and so on.

6 Hold a leg brace against the leg and rail with the narrow edge on the leg, then bradawl pilot holes. Stagger the other brace for that leg as shown, so that the screws do not hit each other. Screw the braces in place, using the 16mm (⅝in) long woodscrews. Repeat for the other legs. To finish, prime and paint the table, and when dry, slide the test tubes into the holes in the top.

Tall shelves

The neat proportions of this shelving unit make it ideal for slipping
into awkward spaces that you otherwise may not use. A design
classic, the shelves are easy both to make and to live with. They
look elegant standing upright, and can also be turned sideways to create
a low-level unit that doubles as a coffee table. Keep the finish simple
with an understated wash of colour that allows the grain of the wood
to show through.

design tips

● Because it can be difficult to cut a true
straight line on large pieces like these with
a hand-held saw, you may prefer to ask
your local timber merchant to cut the
pineboard for you.
● These shelves can be fitted to the wall for
extra stability if required – in children's
rooms, for example. Use flat brass plates,
screws and wall plugs.

Sides
- 2 pieces pineboard 1755 x 315 x 19 mm
  (69 x 12⅜ x ¾ in)

Top, base and shelves
- 4 pieces pine 437 x 315 x 19 mm
  (17¼ x 12⅜ x ¾ in)
- Mitre clamps
- Wood glue
- Power drill with countersink bit
- Countersunk screws
- Screwdriver
- Pencil
- Steel rule
- Wood filler and filling knife
- Sandpaper and sandblock
- Woodstain
- Matt varnish
- Brass plates, screws and wall plugs
  (optional)
- Four castors (optional)

1 Lay one of the side pieces flat and at one end
stand a smaller piece on top and at right angles
to it. Apply wood glue to the meeting edges of
both pieces and secure with a mitre clamp – you
will have to up-end the L-shaped piece and
support the opposite end on a low table or pile of
books until the glue has dried thoroughly. Drill
three equally spaced pilot holes and countersink
screws through the end piece and into the side
piece to secure the joint. Repeat for the opposite
end using the same method. Allow the glue to
dry, then remove the clamps.

2

alternative ideas

- The shelves can be turned on their side and used as a low storage unit and coffee table in one. Simply screw on castors at each corner so that the unit is easy to move around the room.
- You might like to make a set of shelves on a smaller scale than this, as a specific piece of storage, for videos or magazines for example. Make sure that you choose casters that are an appropriate scale for the design.
- The design could easily be adapted to work as a television and video unit or as a low-level divider for a room where two children are sharing. To make it extra safe, invest in castors that incorporate a locking device.

2 To work out the position of the two shelves, measure the inside length of the sides and divide the figure by three. Mark these measurements accurately in pencil on the front and back faces of the sides. Before you fit the shelves, mark half the thickness of each one on the front and back. These marks should align with the pencil marks on the frame. Apply glue to the ends of the shelves and secure them in place with mitre clamps – this will be easier if you stand the piece on its 'legs', as if it was a low table. Continue the pencil line from the shelves across the faces of the side and mark and drill three equally spaced pilot holes. Countersink screw holes and drive in the screws.

3 To attach the second side. apply glue to the edges of the shelves, top and base and place the side in position, making sure that you line up the centre pencil marks. Secure with mitre clamps. When the glue has dried thoroughly, remove the clamps, mark drill holes and countersink three screws through the top and base of each shelf as before. Fill all the screw holes with wood filler, allow to dry and sand smooth with the wood surface.

3

Hinged
mirror

The opulent finish on this mirror
gives it an expensive, designer look
that is irresistibly glamorous. The
metal leaf that creates the
shimmering effect is tricky to handle,
but the end result is impossible to
achieve in any other way.

1 To secure the mirror to the hardboard backing, pack it into position with the four packing strips. Do not use glue to stick the mirror directly onto the board, as not all types of adhesive are compatible with the materials you are using and may react with the mirror. Lay the mirror in place, then apply glue to the bare backing and position the top strip, then one side, the second side and the bottom piece. Use clamps or heavy weights to hold the packing until the glue is dry.

2 Use a pencil and steel rule to mark the rectangular cut-out hole for the mirror on the frame piece of MDF – this should be about 10mm (⅜in) smaller than the mirror, i.e. 450 x 250mm (17½ x 9¾in). Drill holes at each of the four corners, to give the jigsaw clean starting points. Smooth the rough edges with sandpaper.

3 Position the mirror assembly against the back of the frame, then carefully lay both pieces face down on a flat surface, with the backing now on the top. To keep the three sections sandwiched together firmly, you will need to attach a couple of screws at each corner. Measure carefully, however, to make sure that you do not crack the glass, then drill or bradawl small pilot holes. Use 15mm (⅝in) screws so as not to come through the front of the frame. Fill any gaps where the packing strips meet one another with a little wood filler, and sand smooth when dry.

4 To make the doors, measure 60mm (2⅜in) in from the top right corner and the same distance in from the bottom left of the other large piece of MDF. Draw a line between the two points with a steel rule and pencil, and cut along the line with a jigsaw. Sand any rough edges. Lay the frame right side up and place one door on either side, as they would be if opened out. Open the hinges flat, and position them equally and identically on both sides, with one half on the door and the other half on the frame. Draw around the hinges, and use a craft knife to cut shallow rebates so that the four hinges are flush against the MDF.

5 Work carefully when cutting the rebates, so you don't go too deep. Tidy up the rebates, then position the hinges and use a bradawl to make pilot holes for the screws. Screw the hinges securely to each of the doors.

you will need

Frame and doors
- 2 pieces MDF 565 x 365 x 13 mm (22¼ x 14⅜ x ½in)

Backing
- 1 pieces hardboard 565 x 365 mm (22¼ x 14⅜in)

Packing strips
- 2 pieces MDF 360 x 50 x 13 mm (14¼ x 2 x ½in)
- 2 pieces MDF 460 x 50 x 13 mm (18 x 2 x ½in)
- Mirror 460 x 260 mm (18 x 10¼in)
- Power drill with straight bit
- 4 flush hinges, 50 mm (2 in) long, with screws
- 2 picture hanging plates and picture wire
- Gilder's tamping brush or cotton wool
- 2 cuphooks with cord or chain
- Wood filler
- Sandpaper
- Jigsaw
- Craft knife
- Screwdriver
- Clear oil varnish
- G-clamps
- PVA wood glue
- Steel rule and pencil
- Bradawl
- Masking tape
- Size brush
- Metal leaf and size
- Clear oil varnish
- Tack cloth
- Size

6 Depending on your confidence levels and the decorative finish that you plan for the mirror, you can now go one of two ways. If you are going to paint the mirror, screw the other side of the hinge plates to the frame, sand all the MDF, dust off, and apply the paint. If you are planning a more intricate finish or find it easier to work with three small pieces rather than one large one, leave the hinges off the frame for now.

7 Coat all the pieces with a dilute solution of PVA and water at a ratio of around 3:1 to seal them. Leave to dry thoroughly before starting the next step.

8 Draw pencil lines on the inside and outside of each of the doors to act as a guide for positioning the silver leaf squares. These are slightly less the width of a square of metal leaf itself because you overlap the leaf slightly when it is applied. There's no need to draw guide lines on the frame as it is so narrow. Just use your eye to line the leaf up with that on the doors.

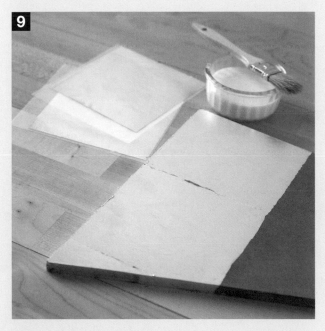

9 You must use special metal leaf size to apply the leaf. Other adhesives simply will not work. Traditional size is oil-based but newer, water-based types are cleaner and much easier to use. Allow a coat of size to become tacky and almost dry to the touch. Take a square of metal leaf transfer and apply it face down on the tacky surface. Rub the backing sheet down using a cotton-wool pad or piece of soft cloth. Carefully peel away the backing sheet and blot the leaf with cotton wool. Continue until you have covered the required area. When the pieces are completely dry, give them a coat or two of an oil-based varnish to seal and protect the delicate surface.

10 Finally, to hold the doors together attach two cuphooks, one to the underside of each of the door. Link these with a length of cord or chain – or anything else that you think may look good.

The Kitchen

No matter what size the kitchen, there never seems to be enough space in it. But help is at hand in the form of three handy pieces of furniture. For tiny kitchens, start with the smallest project and progress onto the next one when you're ready. You'll be amazed at how good these items look – and how much practical difference they will make.

Step stool

Just the right height to help you reach awkward items stored on cupboard tops, this step stool is none the less compact enough to keep in most kitchens or utility rooms. Like all designs inspired by the furniture made by the Shaker communities of the United States, the step stool is not only extremely practical but good to look at too – and you'll find a hundred and one uses for it, both in the kitchen and beyond.

you will need

Sides
- 2 pieces MDF 425 x 405 x 18mm (16¾ x 16 x ¾ in)

Steps
- 2 pieces softwood 515 x 210 x 25mm (20¼ x 8¼ x 1in)

Battens
- 4 pieces softwood 470 x 30 x 30mm (18⅜ x 1⅛ x 1⅛in)
- Jigsaw
- Power drill and straight bit
- Screwdriver
- Wood glue
- Countersunk screws
- Pencil
- Steel rule
- Compasses
- Sandpaper
- Sanding block
- Emulsion paints

● To prevent screws from rusting and showing through on the wood surface, dab a spot of oil-based primer on the heads and leave to dry before filling the holes with wood filler.
● To create a distressed finish on the steps, paint them a medium to dark colour and leave this to dry thoroughly. Next, paint on a lighter colour and when this coat has dried, use sandpaper and a sanding block to remove parts of the top coat, leaving areas of the layer underneath to show through. This creates a weathered, aged effect and looks best when used predominantly on edges, where most wear and tear would show.

1 Trace off the template at the back of the book onto card and draw round it onto both side pieces. Use the jigsaw to cut out this shape to form the legs. Repeat on the other side piece, making sure that the two pieces are identical.

2 The four battens help to strengthen the structure. Lay one side on its inner face and position the battens – one at each of the top two corners, one at the front step and one at the back, just above the curved cut-out. Draw around the battens. Remove the battens and draw diagonal lines between the marked corners of each pencil square on the sides. Drill pilot holes through the MDF where the diagonal lines meet. Apply glue to the batten end, then position it to the drawn square on the inner side face and drive in a countersunk screw through the pilot hole into the batten end.

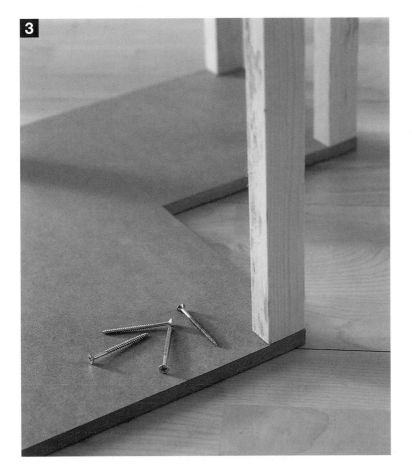

3 Repeat for all four battens, then repeat the whole process for the other side piece. Allow to dry.

4 Position the bottom step, making sure that the overlap is the same on both sides. Mark and drill pilot holes for two screws through the step into the sides, then drive in and countersink the screws. Repeat for the top step.

5 To soften the hard angles, chamfer all the edges and corners with sandpaper wrapped round a sanding block – this will also make the stool safer. Fill all countersunk holes with wood filler, leave to dry and sand smooth.

Plate rack

Ideal for storage and display, this handy plate rack is the perfect finishing touch for kitchens. It makes best use of available space, and can be customized with the addition of a towel rail or screw-in cup hooks. It is heavy, however, so make sure that you get help when fixing it in place.

you will need

Battens
- 3 pieces stripwood 610 x 35 x 22mm (24 x 1⅜ x ⅞in)

Back
- 1 piece MDF 804 x 650 x 13mm (31⅝ x 25⅝ x ½in)

Sides
- 2 pieces softwood 1150 x 310 x 19mm (45¼ x 12¼ x ¾in)

Top
- 1 piece softwood 749 x 310 x 19mm (29½ x 12¼ x ¾in)

Shelves
- 2 pieces MDF 600 x 290 x 12mm (23⅝ x 11⅜ x ½in)
- 1 piece MDF 600 x 327 x 13mm (23⅝ x 12⅞ x ½in)

Shelf supports
- 3 pieces quarter dowelling 600mm (23⅝in) long
- 6 pieces quarter dowelling 280mm (11in) long
- Pencil
- Screws
- Screwdriver
- Jigsaw
- Sandpaper and sanding block
- Power drill and straight bit
- Mitre clamps
- PVA adhesive
- Mitre saw or tenon saw and mitre block
- Hammer
- Panel pins
- Primer and emulsion or eggshell paint
- Varnish

1 On the reverse side of the back board, measure from the base upwards and mark a horizontal line at 15mm (⅜in). From that mark, measure up 315mm (12⅜in) and mark a second line, parallel to the first. Finally, measure up from the second line and mark a horizontal line 260mm (10¼in) from it. These lines give the position of the screw or nail holes that will attach the battens. Next, mark a second line, 6mm (¼in) below and parallel to each of the original lines, to show where the moulding will be attached. To avoid confusion, use different colours for the markings or four pilot screw holes for each batten. Screw or nail the battens in place.

2 Using the template at the back of the book, trace the shaped curve onto the side pieces and cut them out with a jigsaw. Sand to finish and smooth the edges.

3 With sandpaper wrapped around a sanding block, chamfer the edges of the top piece.

4 Lay the two side pieces at either side of the back board and continue the bottom lines (the second set of lines you drew in step 1) across and onto each side. The bottom lines on all three pieces should align. As a guide, mark the thickness of the shelf on the side pieces.

5 To attach the sides to the back, apply glue and secure with mitre clamps as shown – the back of the side pieces should be flush with the battens. Drill and screw through from the outside of the sides into the centre of the battens.

6 Place the top on the sides with an equal overhang at each end and mark the positions. Remove and drill two pilot holes for each side through the top, then apply glue and screw in place.

7 Cut and mitre lengths of quarter dowelling to support the shelves – it is important that you use flat-topped moulding for the shelves to sit securely. Apply glue and nail the three long shelf supports to the back of the plate rack, using the pencil lines as a guide. Attach the six short side supports in the same way.

design tip

● This plate rack is a heavy item of furniture and must be secured safely to the wall. Fix two battens to the wall on which the top two shelf battens can sit, then screw through the shelf battens and into the wall. Use wall plugs for a secure fit.

8 Glue and nail a strip of half-dowelling to the front of the top two shelves – the shallower ones – to prevent plates stored there from slipping off.

9 Slot all three shelves into place. Finish by priming and painting the plate rack, then apply one or two coats of varnish for protection.

Customized shelf

Sometimes making a few additions or adjustments to an existing item can be very effective – and just as satisfying as making something from scratch. Adding a hanging rail to an easily available shelf kit makes it instantly twice as useful as the original item. The transformation takes a few minutes and could hardly be easier – which makes this a great project for beginners.

1 Work out the position of the holes through which the dowelling will be threaded. You need to allow space behind them, so the holes should be on the wide part of the bracket. Mark the centre of the holes. Clamp the brackets together to ensure that the holes align, then use a power-bore drill bit – which needs to be just larger than the diameter of the dowelling – to drill a hole through both brackets.

2 Release the brackets from the clamps, then join the shelf and brackets together following the instructions supplied with the kit. If you feel that extra strength is needed, drill and countersink two screw holes through the top of the shelf into each bracket for extra strength.

3 Chamfer the ends of the dowelling. Thread it through the holes in the brackets. If the dowelling is a little loose, squeeze a little glue into the holes to keep it in place. Fill any screw holes in the top of the shelf, allow to dry and sand flush.

design tips

● The size of the dowelling will depend on the size of the brackets. For large shelves and brackets, consider using larger diameter dowelling.

● For a more contemporary look, replace the dowelling with a chrome or metal pole. These are readily available at DIY stores. Use metal hooks to hang utensils from the pole.

The Bedroom

Bedrooms may need to be everything from a home office to a playroom – as well, of course, as providing somewhere to rest your head at night. A few key items of furniture that solve storage problems, screen off clutter and create an elegant focal point will ensure that your room is a tranquil haven where you can work, rest or play.

Bedhead

This pretty bedhead is simplicity itself and can be adapted for beds of all sizes. Give it a sunbleached look with a pale wash that allows the grain of the wood to show through. A length of cord, threaded through the bed posts and linking two decorative weights, provides an unusual finishing touch.

you will need

- 12 pieces softwood 600 x 70 x 19mm
  (23⅝ x 2¾ x ¾in)
- 1 piece softwood 845 x 70 x 19mm
  (33¼ x 2¾ x ¾in)

Battens

- 2 pieces softwood 904 x 70 x 19mm
  (35⅝ x 2¾ x ¾in)

Posts

- 2 pieces softwood 1340 x 45 x 45mm
  (52¾ x 1¾ x 1¾in)
- Hammer
- Fine nails
- Power drill with 13mm (½in) flat bit and straight bit
- 45mm (1¾in) screws
- Diluted emulsion paint and flat paintbrush
- Cord
- 2 decorative weights
- Needle and coarse thread

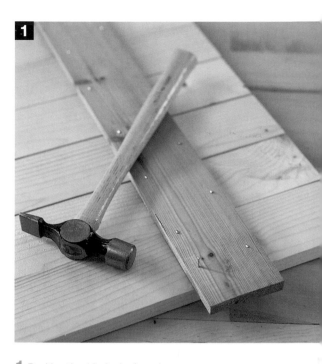

1 Position the 12 planks face down on an even surface, butting them together along their length. Lay the two batten planks horizontally across them at top and bottom, with the edge of the battens 100mm (4in) from the top and base of the planks and overhanging equally on both sides. Hammer in fine nails at regular distances to secure the battens.

2 Mark a line 75mm (3in) from the top of each post, then use a power drill and 13mm (½in) flat bit to drill a hole through each post in the centre of the line.

3 Position the posts along the sides of the planks, with the post tops 150mm (6in) beyond the plank tops. Drill pilot holes through the battens into the posts and drive in 45mm (1¾in) screws to secure.

4 Hammer the remaining pine plank across the bottom edge between the two posts, with its bottom edge flush with the bottom of the planks. Paint the whole bedhead with a wash of diluted emulsion paint and allow to dry completely.

design tip

● You can use anything decorative to weight the cord, as long as it is sufficiently heavy. Pebbles look lovely and are wonderful to the touch – perfect for a seaside bedroom. If you aren't lucky enough to find ones with ready-made holes, you could try making a spiral holding 'cage' from strong wire. Wrap each pebble in wire, working it in a spiral, and loop the end through the cord.

5 Loop the cord through one weight and stitch it in place with coarse thread as shown. Thread the cord through the holes in each post and secure the second weight as before.

Storage box

This unusual box could be put to many uses and makes great low-level storage for anything from bedlinen to shoes or magazines. If you prefer, you can make the box without the legs. For a dramatic finish, experiment with the wonderful metallic paints available in DIY and paint stores.

you will need

Front and back
- 2 pieces MDF
  946 x 310mm x 13mm
  (37¼ x 12¼ x ½in)

Sides
- 2 pieces MDF 310 x 264x 13mm
  (12¼ x 10⅜ x ½in)

Base
- 1 piece MDF 920 x 264 x 13mm
  (36¼ x 10⅜ x ½in)

Lid
- 1 piece MDF 965 x 250 x 13mm
  (38 x 9¾ x ½in)
- 1 piece MDF 965 x 63 x 13mm
  (38 x 2½ x ½in)

Legs
- 2 pieces MDF
  509 x 400 x 25mm
  (19⅝ x 15¾ x 1in)
- Mitre clamps
- PVA adhesive
- Corner braces and screws
- Screwdriver
- 6mm (¼in) D-shaped moulding
- Jigsaw
- Sandpaper and sanding block
- Pencil
- Hammer
- Panel pins
- Power drill and straight bit
- Nails
- 3 decorative hinges and screws
- Primer
- Silver paint and eggshell
  acrylic paint
- Decorative transfers (optional)

1 To attach one side piece to the front, lay the front down flat with a side piece perpendicular at one end. Apply glue along the edge of the side piece and place it on top, then secure with mitre clamps before screwing in two corner braces. Repeat with the back and second side so that you end up with two L-shaped sections.

safety note

- Because the hinged lid is heavy and could slam shut on children's fingers, this item is not suitable for use in a child's room.

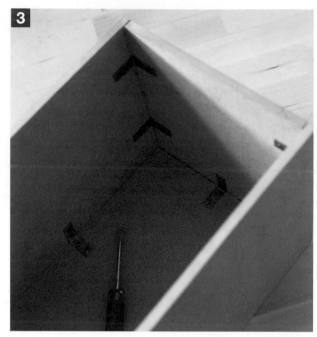

2 Join these two sections together so that you have a rectangular box. Apply glue and clamp, then screw in the corner braces as before.

3 When fitting the rectangular box over the base piece, you cannot slot the base in from the top as the braces will get in the way. Instead, fix the box to the base using glue and two corner braces on each of the long sides, and one at each end.

4 To disguise the joints at the ends of the box, cut D-shaped moulding to length, then apply glue and fix it in position. Secure with panel pins, making sure that the pin heads finish flush with the surface of the moulding.

5 To make the legs, use a photocopier to enlarge the template at the back of the book to the required size. The legs should be 509mm (19⅝in) at the widest point, and the width of the gap should be fractionally larger than 300mm (11¾in) to allow for an easy fit. Trace the template twice onto a large sheet of MDF and cut out the legs with a jigsaw. Sand the edges to finish.

6 Prime both legs, not forgetting the edges. When the primer has dried thoroughly, apply one or two coats of silver-coloured paint.

7 Prime and paint the box itself, using acrylic eggshell. You should also paint both faces of the lid sections at this point, again remembering the edges.

design tips

● Look out for easy-to-use transfers that can transform a plain item of furniture almost instantly. For an understated look, use only a few.
● You can also decorate the box with stamps, stencils or small squares of metal leaf.

9 Join the two lid sections with decorative hinges at equal distances from the ends and in the middle.

8 Stand the box on the legs, then mark and drill pilot holes through the base and sides. You will need two screws in the base and one at either side.

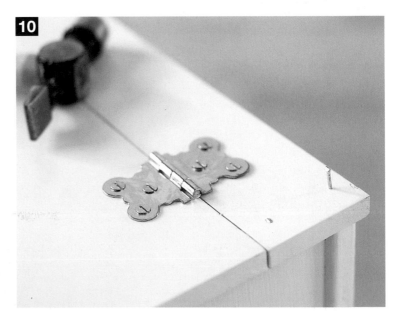

10 Apply glue to the thin lid section along its length and down each short side, then position it accurately on the box. To secure, hammer two nails in at either end and five along the back. Punch in and fill the heads with filler then sand and touch up the paint.

Butler's tray

Based on a traditional design, this updated version of the classic butler's tray is an incredibly handy item and will come in useful time and time again. It can be used in virtually any room throughout the house, and is ideal for serving refreshments in the garden.

you will need

Frame
- 4 pieces stripwood 600 x 18 x 18mm (23⅝ x ¾ x ¾in)
- 2 pieces 8mm (⁵⁄₁₆in) dowelling 355mm (14in) long
- 2 pieces 8mm (⁵⁄₁₆in) dowelling 315mm (12⅜in) long
- 2 pieces 8mm (⁵⁄₁₆in) dowelling 38mm (1½in) long
- Power drill with 8mm (⁵⁄₁₆in) straight bit and flat bit
- Masking tape
- PVA adhesive
- Fabric tape
- Staple gun

Tray base
- 1 piece MDF 509 x 400 x 6mm (19⅝ x 15¾ x ¼in)

Tray sides
- 2 pieces MDF 391 x 80 x 6mm (15⅜ x 3⅛ x ¼in)
- 2 pieces MDF 490 x 80 x 6mm (19¼ x 3⅛ x ¼in)
- Pencil
- Jigsaw
- Mitre saw or tenon saw and mitre block
- Sandpaper and sanding block
- Mitre clamps
- Hammer
- Panel pins
- Primer and emulsion or acrylic paint
- Varnish (optional)
- 2 lengths cord

1 To make the frame, measure 100mm (4in) down from either end of the four pieces of stripwood, mark a line and then mark the centre of the drill hole. Measure 10mm (⅜in) from the tip of the 8mm (⁵⁄₁₆in) drill bit and mark off the rest with masking tape. Drill halfway through each leg – to the edge of the tape on the bit – at the marked point. You should have eight holes in total.

2 Now you need to make two frames, each with two legs and two horizontal dowelling bars. One is slightly narrower than the other, to allow it to slot inside the wider frame, so make sure that the two pieces of dowelling for each frame are the same. Apply glue to the ends of the dowelling and push them into the holes you have drilled.

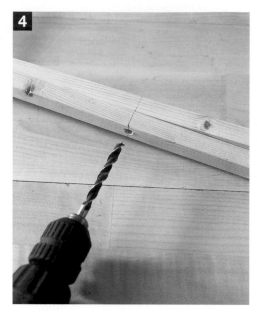

4 Mark the halfway point on each outside leg and find the centre of the outside edge. Remove the tape from the bit and drill through each pair of legs from the outside in.

3 Slot the narrower frame through the wider one so that at one end a narrow dowel is on top and at the other end, underneath. This will enable the frames to pivot.

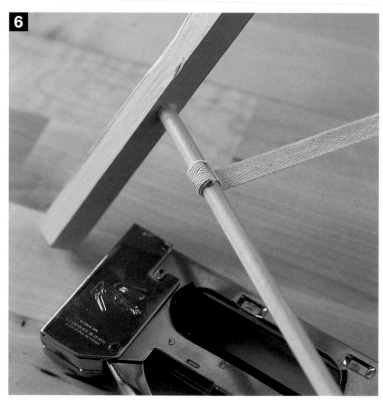

5 Use offcuts from the dowelling to make two 38mm (1½in) long dowel pegs. Hammer these pegs through the holes on either side of each frame from the outside in.

6 Paint the assembled frame. Next, open the frame so that the tray base can be placed on top with room to spare. Measure, cut and staple two lengths of tape to link the top dowelling bars of the two frames, then repeat for the bases.

7 On the tray base, measure in 5mm (³⁄₁₆in) all round the four sides and mark in pencil to make guidelines for positioning the side pieces.

8 Use a mitre saw or tenon saw and mitre block to cut the four side pieces. Check that they will butt up neatly to one another when in place, and sand to fit if required.

9 Use a compass or the template at the back of the book to mark the scalloped edges on the side pieces. Work out how many scallops you want and mark them in place. On the shorter pieces, a single scallop at either side linked by a larger, shallow shape is reasonably uncomplicated to cut out.

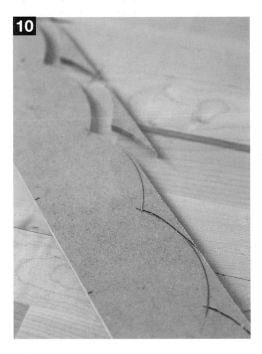

10 Clamp each side in turn and carefully cut out the scalloped edges with a jigsaw. Work a little at a time, starting at the top of each scallop and working down one side of the curve. It's easier to cut the same side of all the scallops before turning and reclamping the sides so that you can cut in the other direction.

11 Use a flat bit to drill holes for the handle cords below the point of the scallop.

12 Apply glue to a long and short side, position and clamp with a mitre clamp to secure, making sure that the mitred edges butt up neatly together. Repeat with the second pair of sides. When the glue has dried thoroughly, join the two L-shaped sections together to form the sides of the tray.

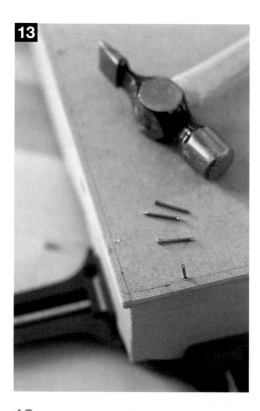

13 Apply glue to the base of the sides and place the base proud of the sides all around. Hammer in panel pins at regular distances, following the pencil lines. Prime and paint the tray then loop the cord through the holes, knotting it on the inside.

Children's Rooms

A child's room is full of design possibilities – and the good news is that the simplest ideas are often the best. Put your new skills to use and brighten up existing furniture, or even create exciting new projects.

Starfish mirror

This fun frame looks great in bedrooms
or bathrooms, and could be adapted
for all sorts of uses. You might like to take
the underwater theme further and
use the template as a basis for a
multi-coloured mural.

you will need

- 1 piece 6mm (¼in) thick MDF
- Pencil
- Circular mirror
- Power drill and straight bit
- Jigsaw
- Sandpaper and sanding block
- Stipple brush
- Emulsion paint
- Bubble wrap
- Small paintbrush
- 2 pieces 18 x 18mm
  (¾ x ¾in) hardboard
- Epoxy resin adhesive
- Small tacks
- Hammer
- Hanging hooks
- Picture wire

1 On a photocopier, blow up the template at the back of the book to the size that you require, using your mirror as a guide to scale. With a pencil, draw around the paper template onto the MDF, then draw a circle in the centre for the mirror. The diameter of the circular hole should be around 10–18 mm (⅜–¾in) smaller than the actual mirror.

2 To cut out the circular centre of the frame, first drill a small hole inside the inner circle and use a jigsaw to cut out the circle anticlockwise (clockwise if you are left-handed). Next, use the jigsaw to cut around the outer edge of the starfish frame. Lightly sand the edges to finish.

4 Fold over a small piece of bubble wrap, with the bubbles on the outside, and coat the surface lightly with a small paintbrush – do not dip the bubble wrap into a tray of paint, as this will ruin the result. Press the painted surface down firmly all around the circular rim to make a narrow band of texture. Then use the same technique to make a tapered band down the centre of each arm.

3 Paint the frame using a stippling brush to give a slightly textured effect. Don't forget to paint the side edges of the MDF too. Allow to dry completely.

5 When the paint has dried, turn the mirror over and on the reverse glue down two small squares of hardboard, at an equal distance on either side of the frame. This is to build up the thickness of the mirror frame so that you can screw in hanging hooks at the end.

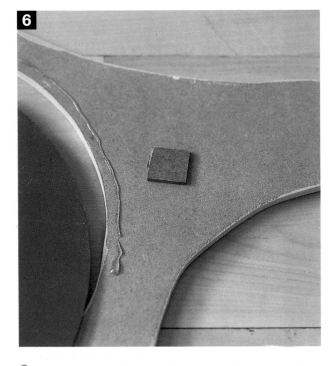

6 Glue the mirror to the back of the frame using epoxy resin adhesive and following the instructions on the packet.

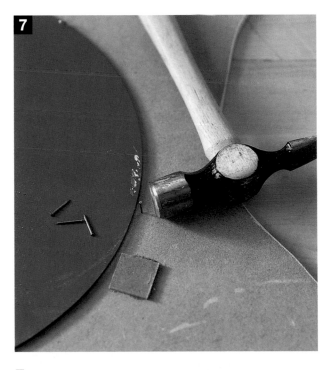

7 To make the mirror extra secure, hammer in small tacks around the edge, starting straight and then knocking them in at an angle towards the mirror to anchor it. Screw the hanging hooks into the hardboard squares, making sure that they do not protrude through the front of the frame. Thread picture wire between the hanging hooks, and the mirror is ready to hang on the wall.

Beach hut screen

Childrens' rooms could always do with more space – but as it is impossible to create extra storage from nowhere, why not do the next best thing, and hide everything that doesn't need to be on display behind a neat little screen? This simple design, painted to look like a row of summer beach huts, is perfect for disguising clutter – and can even double as a little playhouse or theatre.

you will need
- Three pieces of 1220 x 610mm x 13mm (½in) MDF or wood
- Jigsaw
- Sandpaper and block
- Wood glue
- Power drill
- Screwdriver
- Fine nails
- Centre punch
- Bradawl
- Four 405mm (16in) lengths of 10mm (⅜in) quarter-profile moulding
- Four 63mm (2½in) screen hinges
- Masking tape
- Wood filler
- Emulsion paints
- Clear varnish
- Pair of compasses

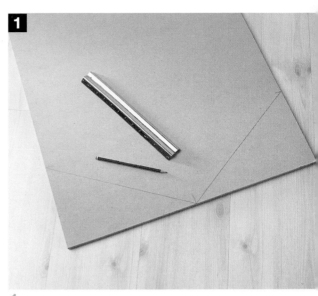

1 To create the roofs, mark in pencil the midpoint, 305mm (12in), on the shorter edge of each piece of MDF or softwood – this is the apex. Now measure 200mm (8in) down on each of the long sides and mark carefully. Ensure that your measuring is accurate or else you may end up with lopsided roofs. Using a steel rule and pencil, draw a line to link each of the side marks with the central mark at the top of each piece.

2 Wearing a mask and goggles, use a jigsaw to cut along the two lines that you have drawn, to form a pointed shape. Do this on each of the three pieces. When you have completed this, use sandpaper wrapped around a wooden or cork sanding block to sand along the newly cut rough edges and give a smooth finish.

3 Measure and mark 815mm (32in) up from the base on each side, then join the lines across. This is the top edge of the window frame. For the bottom edge, measure and mark up 405mm (16in) from the base on each side, then join the marks. For the frame sides, measure and mark 100mm (4in) in along the two lines from each side. Drill a hole at each corner to help you cut cleanly. With a jigsaw, cut out the window, moving from corner to corner.

4 To finish off the window, you need to apply quarter-profile moulding. Cut four 405mm (16in) lengths to fit along the sides of the cut-out square. Glue all the pieces in place, and when the glue has dried, hammer in fine nails along the inner edges of the frame at 100m (4in) intervals. Use a centre punch and hammer to gently tap the nail heads just below the surface of the wood, then fill the holes with a little wood filler and allow to dry completely before gently sanding the filler flush.

5 Prime the front, back and edges of all three pieces of the screen with white emulsion. When the paint has dried completely, measure along the base of each section and mark out the positions of the coloured stripes. The stripes pictured here are around 100mm (4in) wide. Draw the stripes in pencil, using a steel ruler for accuracy. To get a really crisp border for the stripes, firmly apply masking tape along the pencil lines.

6 Lightly draw a horizontal line across the base of each roof, and apply masking tape above the line. For the scalloped decoration, set a pair of compasses to a diameter fractionally smaller than the width of the stripes. Draw the circle on a piece of card and cut in half. Place the straight edge of the template on the guide line and trace the outline of the shape onto each stripe. Paint the scallops in alternate colours. Allow to almost dry, then remove the tape as before and let dry. Erase the guide line. hole. Sand the surfaces.

design tips

● To finish the screen, apply two layers of clear acrylic varnish when the paint has dried, and fit curtains or a blind above the window.
● You can choose stripes of any width, but remember that a narrow design will be trickier to paint.
● In a room that is used by small children, attach one end to the wall with a hook to avoid the screen overbalancing.
● Use different paint effects to create a puppet theatre or play shop.

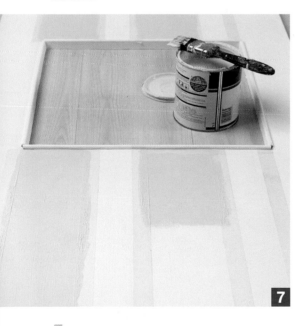

7 Paint on the contrasting stripes with the coloured emulsion, making sure that you cover the surface well – you may need to apply a second coat. At the edges, brush on the paint so that it goes right up to the border and just onto the masking tape – don't flood the edge, or the paint will creep under the tape. Leave the paint until it is almost dry before carefully removing the tape, then touch up any rough edges and allow to dry completely.

8 Lay the central section flat. For the bottom of the lower hinge, mark 150mm (6in) up from the base on each side; for the top of the upper hinge, mark 150mm (6in) down from the top of the scallops. Position the hinges and mark screw holes, leaving the other hole. Mark the screw centres, then insert the screws. Lay one side piece next to the central one, making sure that the bases align. Open the hinges and mark screw holes on the side piece. The edge of the hinge plate should be flush with the edge of the side piece, with the hinge barrel overhanging slightly. Repeat on the other side.

design tip

● This is an excellent way of using up small amounts of emulsion paint that have been left over after decorating a child's room, or any of the painted projects in this book.

Bunting shelves

Plain self-assembly shelving units are easy to pick up for next to nothing – however, though they are undoubtedly useful, they can look utilitarian. So why not give them a quick makeover? These lengths of decorated bunting can be made in a day, and are ideal for beginners to woodwork – and children might even like to lend a hand at the painting stage.

you will need

- 6mm (¼in) thick MDF
- Pencil
- Tenon saw
- Sandpaper and sanding block
- Primer
- Emulsion paints
- Matt varnish
- Upholstery tacks
- Hammer
- Pliers
- Epoxy resin adhesive
- Artist's brush

1 Measure the length of the shelf you want to decorate. Trace the shape of the bunting onto a piece of MDF. Use a tenon saw to cut out the pointed shape. You will find it easiest to start at the bottom point of each triangle and work inwards, cutting first along one of its sides and then the other.

2 Lightly sand the cut edges to finish, brush the dust off and prime the length of bunting.

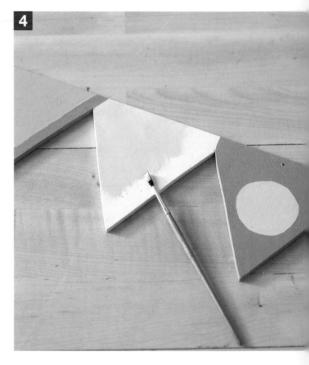

3 Using a pencil, outline the designs that you want to make on each flag. For the best effect, mix a variety of simple designs in a random arrangement.

4 With an artist's brush, fill in the shapes on the primed bunting in three or four shades of paint that will complement your colour scheme. When the paint is completely dry, apply a couple of coats of matt varnish for extra protection.

5 The bunting is secured to the shelving unit with upholstery tacks. Before hammering them in, make three small pilot holes in each piece of MDF. Secure a scrap piece of fabric over the hammer head to protect the surface of the upholstery tack heads.

6 To finish off the piece, cover the screws in the shelving unit with some of the remaining tacks. Cut the pointed ends off with pliers and then glue the upholstery tacks over the screws with a strong adhesive such as epoxy resin.

The Bathroom

A small bathroom can look cluttered if it is filled with different styles of furniture and accessories, so we made these items all in one style for a clean, unified look. The slatted mat that features in all three projects is simplicity itself to make: use spacers to save measuring and get an accurate result every time. The simple paint finish is modern and fresh and further unites the pieces.

Slatted mat

On a tiled or vinyl floor, a slatted wooden bath mat is not only stylish and elegant, but is also more hygienic than an old-fashioned cloth one. If you want to make a longer one, you may need to add another crosspiece to prevent the slats bending.

you will need

Crosspieces
- 3 pieces softwood 410 x 22 x 22mm (16¼ x ⅞ x ⅞in)

Slats
- 8 pieces softwood 610 x 22 x 22mm (24 x ⅞ x ⅞in)

Spacer
- 1 piece MDF 620 x 35 x 13mm (24½ x 1⅜ x ½in)
- 24 galvanized woodscrews 35 x 4mm (1⅜ x ⅛in)
- Pencil
- Try square
- Power drill and 4mm (⅛in) straight bit
- Screwdriver
- Emulsion paint
- Rag
- Polyurethane varnish
- Paintbrush

1 On one of the crosspieces, mark off divisions with the spacer and one of the slats. Lay the slat across the crosspiece, flush with the end, and draw a pencil line. Remove the slat, lay the spacer against the pencil line and draw another line. Continue marking alternate slat and spacer divisions right down the crosspiece, ending with a slat, which should be flush with the end. Align the other two crosspieces with the marked one and, using a try square, continue the pencil lines across all the crosspieces.

2 Fit a 4mm (⅛in) straight bit into a power drill and drill a hole through the centre of each slat space on all three crosspieces. To find the true centre, draw diagonal lines between the corners of the slat spaces.

- A matching soap dish is simple to make: simply use two crosspieces and five slats, and reduce all the dimensions accordingly, including the screws (or use panel pins), and assemble in the same way.
- Experiment with two washes of different colours on a piece of scrap wood – if you like the effect, use it on the finished mat.

3 Lay one of the slats on a flat surface and position the crosspieces at right angles on top of it, the ends of the crosspieces flush with the side of the slat. To keep the crosspieces level, put another slat under the far end. One crosspiece should lie exactly across the middle of the slat, and the others should align with each end. Use a bradawl to mark down through the pre-drilled hole in each cross piece into the slat before screwing the two end ones first, then the middle one.

4 Lay the spacer under the crosspieces, flush against the slat. Push the next slat up against the spacer, then bradawl and screw down through the holes as before. Continue in this way until all the slats are attached to the crosspieces. For a limewashed look, wipe the wood with a rag soaked in diluted white emulsion paint. When dry, seal with two coats of polyurethane varnish.

Bathroom storage unit

This wonderfully useful unit is based on the traditional butler's tray, but adapted to the needs of the modern bathroom. The shelf is the basic slatted bath mat, while the top provides clever storage space for toiletries.

1 Measure up 22mm (⅞in) from the bottom of both long and both short sides, and use a straight edge to draw a line between the marks.

you will need

Base
- 1 piece MDF 582 x 280 x 18mm (22⅞ x 11 x ¾in)

Sides
- 2 pieces MDF 600 x 88 x 10mm (23⅝ x 3½ x ⅜in)
- 2 pieces MDF 280 x 88 x 10mm (11 x 3½ x ⅜in)

Dividers
- 2 pieces MDF 280 x 50 x 10mm (11 x 2 x ⅜in)
- 3 pieces MDF 188 x 50 x 10mm (7⅜ x 2 x ⅜in)

Lid tops
- 3 pieces MDF 195 x 145 x 10mm (7¾ x 5¾ x ⅜in)

Lid bases
- 3 pieces MDF 185 x 135 x 10mm (7¼ x 5¼ x ⅜in)

Legs
- 4 pieces softwood 532 x 22 x 22mm (20⅞ x ⅞ x ⅞in)

Crosspieces
- 2 pieces softwood 280 x 22 x 22mm (11 x ⅞ x ⅞in)

Slats
- 5 pieces softwood 540 x 22 x 22mm (21¼ x ⅞ x ⅞in)

Spacer
- 1 piece MDF 560 x 425 x 10mm (22 x 16¾ x ⅜in)
- Woodscrews:
- 10 galvanized 35 x 4mm (1⅜ x ⅛in)
- 4 galvanized 50 x 4mm (2 x ⅛in)
- 4 galvanized 40 x 4mm (1⅝ x ⅛in)
- Pencil, straight edge and try square
- PVA wood glue and wood filler
- Hammer and panel pins
- Power drill with 4mm (⅛in) straight bit and 25mm (1in) spade bit
- Screwdriver and bradawl
- Abrasive paper and sanding block
- Emulsion paint and polyurethane varnish

2 One side at a time, run a line of wood glue along an edge of the base and lay a side piece against it, with the pencil line level with the bottom of the base. Do the short sides first, then the long sides to make a tray.

3 Make sure that the base and sides meet at right angles, then hammer panel pins through each side at a time into the edge of the base, spacing them at roughly 75mm (3in) intervals. Allow the glue to dry.

4 Measure and draw a line lengthways down the middle of the tray. Use two of the short dividers as spacers to set the position of the first long divider across the tray. Position the spacers as shown, put in the long divider and draw a pencil line down each side of it. Remove the long divider, leaving the short dividers in place.

5 Run a line of wood glue along the bottom and side edges of a long divider and stand it between the pencil lines in front of the short dividers. Check for right angles and leave to dry. Remove the short dividers and, working from the other end of the tray, use them to position the second long divider in the same way.

6 One section at a time, run a line of wood glue along the bottom and side edges of a short divider and stand it on the lengthways pencil line, then leave to dry. Hammer two panel pins through the sides of the tray into the each end of the four dividers that touch the sides of the tray. Mark a hole 13mm (½in) in on a diagonal from each corner of the top of the base, then use a straight bit to drill a hole.

8 Find the centre of each lid top by drawing two diagonal lines between the corners – the point where they meet is the centre. Drill a hole right through the centre of the lids with a power drill and 25mm (1in) spade drill bit.

7 Position the lid bases on the tops so they are central, then mark round the bases with a pencil. Remove the bases, apply wood glue to them and fix them firmly into position. Allow to dry.

9 Make up a slatted shelf in the same way as the slatted mat on page 98, but with only two crosspieces, one at each end.

10 Mark a hole 200mm (8in) up from the bottom of each leg, then use a straight bit to drill through the legs. Working one leg at a time, apply wood glue to the top of the leg and to the top 19mm (¾in) of two sides. Position the leg in a corner of the underside of the tray, with the glued sides against the edges of the tray and the pre-drilled hole facing into the centre of the tray. Rest the other end of the leg on the shelf spacer to hold it level.

11 Screw down through the hole in the top of the tray into the top of the leg. Attach the other legs in the same way.

12 Position the slatted shelf between the legs, level with the pre-drilled holes, bradawl through into the shelf and screw through the legs into the end grain of the slats.

13 Fill and sand all screw holes. Prime the tray and lids then paint the inside of the tray with emulsion. Drag the outside of the tray and the tops of the lids by soaking a rag with diluted emulsion paint and wiping it over the surface. Drag the legs and slatted tray with diluted white emulsion in the same way to give a limewashed look. Seal the whole unit with two coats of polyurethane varnish.

Peg rail

Places to put flannels, towels and other bathtime accessories are always welcome, even in large bathrooms. This peg rail solves the storage problem with a minimum of fuss and completes the matching set to give your bathroom a touch of class.

you will need

Crosspieces ● 2 pieces softwood 290 x 22 x 22mm (11⅜ x ⅞ x ⅞in)

Slats ● 6 pieces softwood 600 x 22 x 22mm (23⅝ x ⅞ x ⅞in)

Spacer ● 1 piece MDF 610 x 35 x 13mm (24 x 1⅜ x ½in)

Rail back board ● 1 piece softwood 600 x 145 x 18mm (23⅝ x 5⅝ x ¾in)

Pegs ● 4 wooden dowels 120mm (4¾in) long and 25mm (1in) diameter

Brackets ● 2 pieces softwood 110 x 110 x 19mm (4⅜ x 4⅜ x ¾in)

Back bars ● 2 pieces softwood 330 x 45 x 19mm (13 x 1¾ x ¾in)

● 20 galvanized woodscrews 35 x 4mm (1⅜ x ⅛in)

● Pencil

● Straightedge

● Try square

● Power drill with 4mm (⅛in) straight bit and 25mm (1in) spade bit

● Screwdriver and bradawl

● Abrasive paper and sanding block

● Wood glue and wood filler

● Emulsion paint

● Polyurethane varnish

1 Make up a slatted shelf in the same way as the slatted mat on page 98, this time using only two crosspieces, one at each end.

2

2 Draw a pencil line lengthways across the middle of the rail back board. Make a pencil mark on this line 75mm (3in) in from each end and then two more marks 150mm (6in) in from the first two. Drill a hole at each marked point with a 25mm (1in) spade bit.

3

3 Chamfer the ends of each piece of dowel.

4

4 Apply PVA wood glue around the end of each piece of dowel and push it to fit firmly into the drilled holes in the back board. Check that the pegs are at right angles to the board and leave to dry.

5 Cut two brackets to size and then place one against each back bar, flush with the top and aligned against opposite sides. Mark the position and use the 4mm (⅛in) straight bit to drill two pilot holes from the back of each bar into the bracket. Insert the screws and tighten them.

6 Mark 22mm (⅞in) in from each end of the back board. Use the 4mm (⅛in) straight bit to drill two pilot holes from the back of each bar into the board. Screw into position.

7 Position the shelf on the brackets, with the top of each bracket flush with the inside of the crosspieces. Drill two pilot holes through each bracket into the crosspieces and screw in place – check first that the screws will not hit the screws holding the slats to the crosspieces. Fill all screw holes with wood filler and sand flush when dry. For a limewashed look, wipe the wood with a rag soaked in diluted white emulsion paint. When dry, seal with two coats of polyurethane varnish.

The Garden

Whether you are a keen gardener or simply view your garden as an extra, outdoor room, everyone enjoys being outside when the weather is fine. Now you can add to that enjoyment with these simple projects that have a distinctly designer look – but which cost considerably less to make than mass-produced, shop-bought items.

Garden bench

Make the most of summer weather with this smart garden bench. It's simple to put together, so after you've got the hang of how to make it, experiment with different sizes and colours to create a versatile range of outdoor furniture that will grace any garden.

you will need

Top
- 1 piece pine
  1219 x 267 x 25mm
  (48 x 10½ x 1in)

Sides
- 2 pieces pine
  1219 x 255 x 25mm
  (48 x 10 x 1in)

Legs
- 2 pieces pine
  355 x 260 x 25mm
  (14 x 10¼ x 1in)
- Galvanized screws and nails
- Jigsaw and pencil
- Drill and straight bit
- Sandpaper and sanding block
- Mitre clamps
- Wood filler
- Exterior wood stain

1 To make the notches in each leg, measure along the base (the 267mm/10½in edge) of each leg to find the midpoint, mark it, then divide the section on either side in two so that the leg is divided into four. Now measure around 120mm (4¾in) up from the midpoint and mark. At this point, drill a hole to form the apex of the cut-out notch. Find the quarter sections marked on the base and cut out the triangular section with a jigsaw. Each time, start at the base and work towards the drilled hole. Sand the newly cut surfaces thoroughly.

2 Now you need to attach the legs to the top of the bench. Around 120mm (4¾in) in from each end of the top, mark a line on the underside. These lines should be parallel to the ends and to each other. Glue and clamp the legs in place. For extra security, when the glue has dried, turn the bench over and drill three holes through the seat into each leg and punch in 50mm (2in) galvanized nails. Fill the holes with wood filler and sand down when dry.

3 To attach the two sides, first angle the corners with a jigsaw. To ensure a neat finish, place each side against the bench and mark on the outer edges the thickness of the top section. After cutting, sand thoroughly. Countersink five holes along each side section. The two outer holes should be around 75mm (3in) in from the sides. Screw each side onto the bench, then drill two additional holes over each leg section and screw in place.

4 If your bench is for outdoor use, finish it with a wood stain or paint recommended for garden furniture – and don't forget to coat the underside of the legs. For indoor use, you can get away with a coat or two of emulsion. Either way, give the bench a weathered look by lightly sanding the outer edges between coats.

Planter covers

Plastic troughs are an inexpensive way of displaying colourful flowers and foliage, but they don't look very inspiring. These simple, wooden slip-over covers transform plastic planters in an instant and can be swapped around to coordinate with different plants and colours. The sizes given here are to match standard plastic troughs.

you will need

FRONT AND BACK
- 2 pieces softwood 930 x 650 x 13mm (36⅝ x 25⅝ x ½in)

SIDES
- 2 pieces softwood 600 x 650 x 13mm (23⅝ x 25⅝ x ½in)
- Jigsaw
- Pencil
- Tracing paper
- Sandpaper and sanding block
- Mitre clamps
- 8 corrugated fastenings
- Hammer
- Coloured exterior woodstain

1 Choose a template design from the ones at the back of the book. Increase it to the correct dimensions for your cover using a photocopier. Cut out the template and draw around it to transfer the design onto the front and back pieces of your cover. Cut the pieces out carefully with a jigsaw, and sand to finish the edges.

2 Clamp the front and sides together using a couple of mitre clamps. You should inset the sides very slightly – around 10mm (⅜in) or so is ideal.

design tips

● Adapt the design to suit the size of your planter – or why not come up with a template of your own?
● Because these covers have no base, you don't have to worry about drainage. They simply slot over the top of plastic troughs to give the appearance of a wooden window box or planter.

3 Hammer in corrugated fastenings at a diagonal across the top and bottom of each join to secure. Attach the back piece in the same way and finish off with a coloured woodstain specially formulated for outdoor use.

Bamboo planter

This planter is exteremely inexpensive to make – and doesn't require much in the way of special tools or materials. You will need to be patient, however, as some of the steps are a bit fiddly. Take your time, and you'll be rewarded with a handsome-looking garden container that's a true original.

you will need

- Stripwood 22 x 22mm (⅝ in x ⅝ in)
- Saw or jigsaw
- Mitre clamps
- 3.5mm (⅛ in) panel pins
- Glue gun and glue sticks
- Bamboo

1 To make the basic frame of the planter, you will need to make one square to form the top and another for the base. These are each made from two 355mm (14in) lengths and two 260mm (10¼in) lengths. With this method there's no need for mitred corners. Glue and clamp the wood to form the frames, and secure with panel pins as shown. Leave to dry thoroughly.

2 Now join the top and bottom by attaching the four leg sections to create a 'box'. The top of each leg should come halfway up the inside of the upper frame. Use wood glue and panel pins to secure as before. Fit the bottom frame over the legs after the top section is in place.

3 Next you need to attach the slats to the base of the planter. Place the frame top down and butt a slat up to each pair of legs, then space the remaining slats around 16mm (⅝in) apart. Attach each one with wood glue and a panel pin at each end.

4 Now you're ready to attach the bamboo. Before you start, cut plenty of lengths to size – you'll be surprised at how much you use. Clean the bamboo thoroughly by wiping with white spirit or sugar soap solution to ensure that the glue adheres properly. Now attach each stick of bamboo, top and bottom, with a dab of hot glue from a glue gun. If you haven't got a glue gun, you can use ordinary wood glue – but be prepared to wait a little longer for the glue to dry.

p28 Letter Rack

p72 Storage box

p76 Butler's tray

p54 Step stool

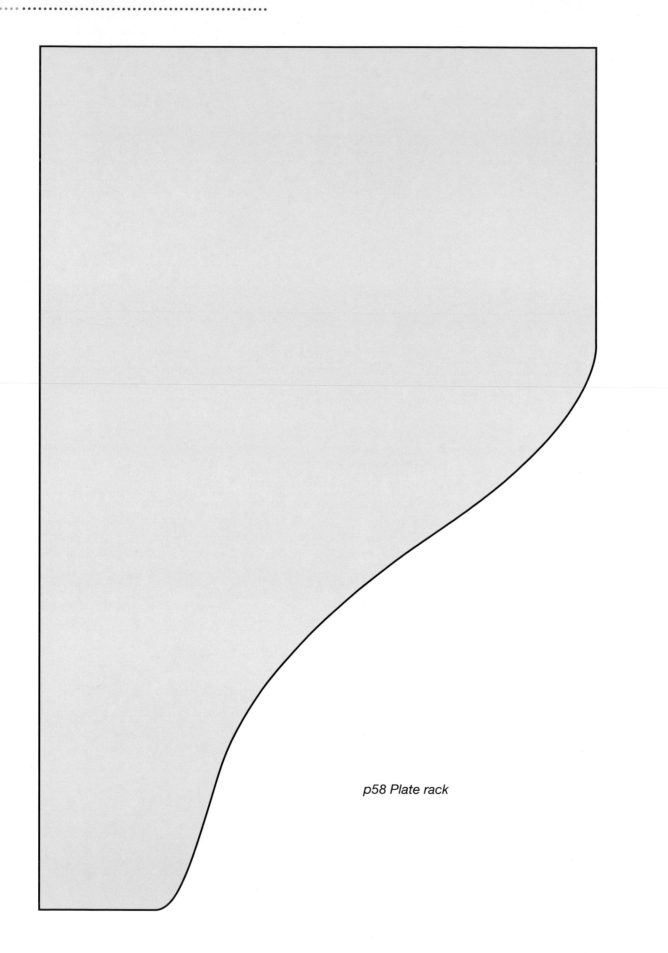

p58 Plate rack

p84 Starfish mirror

p116 Planter covers

Glossary

Arris A sharp edge where two surfaces meet at an angle

Batten A strip of wood, often used to describe wood attached to a wall for holding a component in place

Bevel Any angle, other than a right angle, cut on a piece of wood or found on a tool blade; to cut such an angle

Chamfer A small 45-degree bevel,planed along the edge of a piece of wood to make it less sharp; to plane such a bevel

Check A split in the surface of wood as a result of unequal drying

Chipboard A coarse-finished man-made board, often faced with melamine laminate or hardwood veneer and used in inexpensive furniture and kitchen units

Counterbore A hole drilled into wood to allow the entire head of a screw or bolt to end up below the surface; to drill such a hole

Cross grain Grain that does not follow the main grain direction in a workpiece

Cup On a piece of wood, to bend, usually across the width, as a direct result of shrinkage

Dowel A short, round length of wood that is fitted into holes in two pieces of wood to hold them together; to fit such a piece

Dowelling A long length of wood for dowelling, often used for decoration, in plate racks, etc.

Dry-assembling Fitting together or assembling workpieces without fixing or gluing them, to check for an accurate fit and that all angles are true before final fixing

End grain The irregular surface of wood that is exposed after cutting across the fibres

Face edge The surface planed square to the face side

Face side On a piece of wood, the flat surface (usually planed) from which all measurements

and angles are taken

Fence A device attached to a workpiece or tool to enable a straight line to be cut parallel to the edge of the wood – proprietary fences are available for many power tools, but they can be home-made

Galvanized Screws or nails covered with a protective layer of zinc, used to prevent rusting in outdoor projects

Grain The direction or alignment of the fibres in a piece of wood

Groove A narrow channel cut along a piece of wood in the direction of the grain; to cut such a channel

Hardboard A slightly flexible man-made board, mostly used for the back panels of shelves, cabinets, etc.

Hardwood Wood that comes from deciduous, broad-leafed trees – not necessarily harder than softwood

Hone To sharpen the edge of a blade and create the final cutting edge on it

Jig A device, often home-made, for holding a piece of work in position and enabling repeated working to be done on it

Kerf The cut made in wood by a saw

Knock-down (KD) fitting A metal or plastic fitting for joining two pieces of wood at right angles. KD fittings are designed to be easily taken apart, and are mostly used in flat-pack and kitchen furniture

Laminate A flat surface made by bonding different layers together, such as plastic, melamine, etc.; to make such a board

Marine plywood or board A plywood made with water-resistant hardwood layers and strong glue, used for exterior projects and those where moisture and condensation may occur

Medium-density fibreboard (MDF) A versatile, smooth-surfaced man-made board, produced by binding wood dust together with glue

Mitre A corner joint for which two pieces of wood are cut with bevels of equal angles, usually 45 degrees; to cut such a joint

Moulding A length of wood, either hardwood or softwood, that has a shaped profile

Offcut A piece of scrap wood left over after a workpiece has been cut or shaped

Pare To remove fine shavings from a piece of wood by hand-manipulation of a chisel

Patina The subtle colour and texture acquired by timber as it ages

Pilot hole A small hole drilled into wood that acts as a guide for the thread of a woodscrew

Planed all round (PAR) A length of wood or plank that has has all four sides planed before being sold – the dimensions given, however, are for the wood before it was planed, so a PAR length will be smaller than these

Planed two sides (P2S) A length of wood or plank that has had two opposing sides planed before being sold

Plasterboard A man-made board where two layers of thick paper or card sandwich a layer of plaster – used to make cavity walls

Plywood A strong man-made board produced by gluing thin layers of board together – often faced with hardwood or softwood veneer

Primer The first coat of paint on bare wood, designed to seal the surface and provide a base for subsequent coats

Rebate A recess, step or groove, usually rectangular, that is cut into a piece of wood to allow a mating piece to be inserted

Size A weak solution of glue – in woodworking, used mainly in applying metal leaf or similar

Skew Describes a nail or screw that is driven in to one or more pieces of wood at an angle other than a right angle; to drive in a nail or screw in this way, usually intentionally

Slat A narrow, usually thin, length of wood used as part of an identical series to form a fence, chair seat and back, etc.

Softwood Wood that comes from coniferous trees – not necessarily softer than hardwood

Splitting out The result of a cutter or bit cutting through the other side opposite the face side

Stile The vertical side pieces of a door or window frame

Stock The main body or handle of a tool, usually made of hardwood or plastic

Tang The sharp, pointed end of a chisel or rasp that is driven into the stock or handle

Template A pattern or shape, usually drawn on card, paper or thin board, used as a guide for accurate marking on wood or man-made boards, especially when more than one identical piece is required

Tongue-and-groove A joint in which a thin tongue of wood on one piece of wood is fitted into a matching groove on another – mainly used in doors and wall panels

True Describes when something is exact, e.g. a true right angle is perfectly accurate; to smooth perfectly flat with a plane, chisel or sander

Winding Describes a warped or twisted length of wood

With the grain Working wood along the direction or alignment of the fibres

Workpiece A piece of wood or project that is unfinished and still being worked on